The Banjo Clock

KAREN GARTHE

The Banjo Clock

 University of California Press   Berkeley Los Angeles London

NATIONAL
ENDOWMENT
FOR THE ARTS

This project is supported in part by an award from the National Endowment for the Arts.

University of California Press, one of the most distinguished university presses in the United States, enriches lives around the world by advancing scholarship in the humanities, social sciences, and natural sciences. Its activities are supported by the UC Press Foundation and by philanthropic contributions from individuals and institutions. For more information, visit www.ucpress.edu.

University of California Press
Berkeley and Los Angeles, California

University of California Press, Ltd.
London, England

Library of Congress Cataloging-in-Publication Data

Garthe, Karen, 1949–.
    The banjo clock / Karen Garthe.
        p.   cm. — (New California poetry ; 34)
    Includes bibliographical references.
    ISBN 978-0-520-27316-0 (pbk. : alk. paper)
    I. Title.
    PS3607.A777B36   2012
    811'.6—dc23   2011043106

Manufactured in the United States of America

21   20   19   18   17   16   15   14   13   12
10   9   8   7   6   5   4   3   2   1

The paper used in this publication meets the minimum requirements of ANSI/NISO Z39.48-1992 (R 2002) (*Permanence of Paper*).

To my champion

'The door opens,' says the language that doesn't say 'someone opens the door.' Is it mother, is it cat, is it wolf, is it you?

HÉLÈNE CIXOUS

Contents

3   *Fanta grape*

4   Rid the kitchen

5   Ikebana

6   Gorge

7   Ink Runs

8   REHAB (we want grace walls)

9   National sky

10   Buckle up, Sweetie

11   *Piranesi under The Keystone of A*

12   *Eternal Youth*

13   PARTITA *Flat-out Mars*

14   To *Dolls Big as Clara*

16   Bear

17   *Dolly Loves the Ocean*

18   Little Soulyard, 1

19   Island of the Judge who kept us

20   State Fair

21   First surge Cable

22   my *Liebestod*

23   *Frail of a year*

24   Midwest

25 soldiering PARTITA

27 Little Soulyard, 2

29 Sadly, I noticed

32 Andrew, all bespoke

33 The Porticos of Toulouse

35 Porn Guy *Idée Fixe*

37 Champagne Blondes / Little Scrap of Irony

39 The Challenge

40 59th Street Station

41 Sweet Thing Theology

42 To the Cinematographer

45 High Nouns Shepherd

46 *Speak Revenue*

47 *mantra*

48 Solace Ritual

50 The Dark Dauphine

51 A Letter from Home *To Karen Dalton*

52 *Call Sleeping*

53 The Chiffon Artist

54 Beauty

55 Mandarin Character, YELLO CROWN

56 Water Quip

58 *Poem on Velvet* & Fire's Extra Fun

60 djinns in orbit

61 14 lines

62 2 hands writing

63 Blue Hour

64 Great Expectations

66 Great North Primitive Story

68 Bread Alone

69 *Poem on Velvet,* Carnegie Hall

70 Floating Island

71 Red Sleep

72 WIDOW   on a train

74 Outside's

75 *Baby Krishna crawls to bliss*

76 The Banjo Clock

79 *Acknowledgments*

81 *Notes*

The Banjo Clock

Fanta grape

I was tasting the Molotov vapor
wick-soaked gasoline
furthering its career
hoisted to meet the numb cold permanently
jingling coins and oily paper money
lasting outlasting debris
smacking my tongue to its tusks
dipped in a *Fanta grape*
thumbed at the top shaking

Rid the kitchen

What'll I do to repair the mines and files of a breach of a hundred anemic fadings
                    features rattled
            and so harmed
        warehouse motes   huddles I sang to
        cold blood   twangy raw ends   spit of crazy rolled over
                                the lot
              the warehouse   row of shoes
          I found
        the suicide on the desk
& the contraption I know as the only thing to be awed by
due diligence

Ikebana

Another sleeping limo driver and too much guessy
Lowdown
Overnaming, hopping the magnification of any resemblance to 100%

The way "call another boom delivery" costs more than itself

      A biding sparkle, wry barbell maintenance

      Finally, to add the *craquelure* of beauteous scarring

A small common tool that comes into clear view without its task and

      The motion of new utility

Gorge

Baleen torqued hipped Gorge

turned in drying stiffening

working up to its crevasse

Looming
rippled blues
of what to feed the fathoms but take one's time
dark passes

gimps on clever
recedes as from out-of-style consciousness, out-of-style rescue

scarlet enmities/pieties cruise

This, your playmate
This, your fill
of plebiscites whiskered to yello age
plump
rosy permanents

stun these sharpshooters
this wall with its crevasse

Ink Runs

Ink Run *damn ink*
with its bit-play on startle the temporary lease curls
     its glycerin, its fancy quiver
                              bears struggles, repeat: *struggles*
          down quibbling sludge eddies and mercury bumps
transport warmed from holding the quiet, repeat
          The Quiet sinking down moves on

REHAB (we want grace walls)

Something to it, a line to start rehab and democratize the body's
frail thrashings
waterslapping deletions
This skyline's Beijing's dovecote but destination *Song of America Cartoon*
                                        A wide-eyed midge,
                        the heroine's flight to restore
bulging Popeye, coy Betty mincing her pinpoints
shrugging
            Oh! Oh! What do we want?
            to the distance that quits her as she'll quit others

Crescendo: *I got a message from my love in the ocean, there in the water
            particled by sound*
        a line to start the journey beach-cheap . . . Beijing-style
                                        Towers
                                        Tiles
                                        Totems
To haul frail deletions, bedside adorables as kittens sweet in their buttons
            to the monstrous frail
                    Tenderize their water
                    And their air
            the Future Gates
the iron dollops of *We want grace walls*
easy maintenance

National sky

far spicy arithmetic, petals of
Sugar in the coffee day
rasher
of national sky, yellowing dates hang their chits in atmosphere
zone the yellowing
news and debris
shrimp tin in the sink
a mug of memorabilia's
pinless grenade
more ash than saying THE FOG IN A BLEND OF SIMPLES escalating fugue
not a cloying phobic or a sad brown nettle
just the hustle of weightless
furrowing thru tinkling empties, clank of a full can
Trying
Managing
wiles grayed down from an unseen flipping point
pivot the speaker
in maize more green than stalwart
more
innocently stalled
and far more breached and dismayed

Buckle up, Sweetie

glory *wreathes, flutes*
to Corinthian foliage, the heavy tops of stone
                    Who is crying
            and holding her eyes?
Whose impervious listens? Stick tables and chairs bite gravel

            Would Harry talk to Jane if
she didn't have money? Whose della Robbia,
whose travertine Brahms
demotic
double-teams the gorgeous transvestite?

                    Buckle up, Sweetie
and keep a stable chronology
the demonstrative kindness of elderly shut
night
figments, and early modes of play

Piranesi
under
    The Keystone of A

You must feel warmed by Helen's small fires   by inscription as vine and

Episode   Fragments

You must converse in a niche to the doll's effigy

By Helen's you must feel warmly a pillow decanting   widow tea drops

Pale for the linen the sky pushed formally jellies on

Armies surrounding the largo base and Piranesi numbering the plates

The wedding cake tier undoing

Doorways   arbors

Augustan seizures   mounds gnawed filigree and bricksworn sibilant hours

Walk the lion scourge precisely

Eternal Youth

J Gandy's drawn candled vaulting sepulcher Mortuaries of Giza's little
groundstones

lift here like money *the scarred back sways* coins groan in their vitrine

and Elizabeth House-on-Thames performs the ink of the river of truth

is stones paunch

with gout inevitability

Who passed away? Platforms sanguine and Uch tombed in the Mughal style

that troglodyte feeling only comfy in the dark

the student of Bath's circus oyster plates constellate

a plumb line and none of dreaming *Here* was *their best friend*

and their sadness robin redbreast tall

is not for food

at least not for us

lace makers and weavers Youth eyes webbing pruning the cortege

the scarred back sways the chewed tombs in Uch in Mughal glazed ceramics

the head toss The air tray

PARTITA *Flat-out Mars*

Jelly spoon on the dash and a pinafore dress
Aura of Drive blessing the river   color-drenched
Red Mars
Bloodglass
Exeunt or arriving best known/best alone
glazes
the heel-toe scattershells   the aircrafts of moisture
phenomenon

Why are Gnostic frost, lavender bedecking the psychic pain
fascia off the bone warden
antic/icon poses
adjusting mere chin straps, boots
marrying all gloss, gripping the skin around us
Aircrafts of moisture
Fomenting
archipelagoes
canary bright pickets
jewelling zealous
folds
the *Aura of Drive*
God speeds
Mars

To *Dolls Big as Clara*

Between a gown and an opera curtain
Herr Drosselmeyer's best at
keeping children
children
and the Tudor witch hats grade so the lids won't pool
to soggy ruin
Thus, Herr Drosselmeyer
and the mischief of all true things
to dolls big as Clara
whose cloaks of invisibility
secretly light the sock drawers, the mud room
hills of brogue, chrysanthemum pom
the gardener missing
weeds of his old retractable lease
and Drosselmeyer
finger-wagging
inscrutably
but still keeping children
children
still shoring the stones up
in their rock place
and turrets for frivolity,

and for spirit . . . The Great Witched Pitches
two dolls get up to
smoothing their gowns
and no one pooled to soggy ruin

Bear

Hibernating bear
Hunting bear
naked skin north fishing bear Companion
in starry mineral veins
warm brown
Bear
Swimmer
kelp lace

Buoyed mail order bride bear's wedding cackle through the piney
pristine
rolled sleep
den bear
Pungent
Emergent

      Rock corridor *What kind of fish can these bony*
        wickers
     boggy irons
after all hibernal oils?

      Hut
      &
      veldts
When first my father settled here,
  'Twas then the frontier line:
The panther's scream, filled night with fear
  And bears preyed on the swine.

Dolly Loves the Ocean

spreads like a blood wound
seeps face-up and mutes
                                the sky where she flings her
love salts failing
the sharp-hipped sycamore sheds
magnanimous crooks the township maples and ice
                                Dolly's plastic no-face
                                littles
                                        the glass
but Dolly Loves the Ocean, her cheek moping the frame
the great dollop of consequence deep bells clang

Dolly loves

pastry crenellate and nuclear frond sounds off the radio
plaintive scrappling, tumbling
curls of the ocean's tumbled curls

Little Soulyard, 1

Light for myself and ever after
characters in clear air
are cold shabby dolls'
pale skirts
bruised pinions

Appalachian death song the hawk swoops bare trees

Little dragoons of vision moored in unforgiving whilst appearing to forgive

Sorrow without decoration

The upset clouds
The archaic family's
notion
of order
in the bargain

Of
winter frugalities
extreme
cold doll
bare trees

Island of the Judge who kept us

at the portal's extreme Xanadu cave who's Trusted God in this
nebbish with a rude cold

HERE HERE'S "Too-Chic-To-Live" and many Old Time
Social Workers plow for good

on the candified granite plenty of swirling
contradiction rings

sex crimes
jiffy pills that kick

gray thin news and the festival tropical juices
in womanish anachronous

plastic shapes, bio-frills and involuntarily reflex
The Same Dream Query

though explained within the dream
never explains the dream itself

   (was the second sharp island of the Judge who kept us)

I don't know how I dreamt it but I did and
I was wrong

I folded her in sheets in Xanadu
at the portal in the fallen asleep spheres of the room

how my hands hurt I thought
this livid spleen

State Fair

He opens a thousand windows and he closes a thousand curtains
He could have easily guessed this.
I tried not to annex you for just my country.
I tried to bring him in. I put my head in Jen's lap
About the new languish. If it's jinxed already
You've got to let go. It's zero hour she said
You have no idea.
They must have heard when the Ferris wheel bolted . . .
Here's how they stand around at the State Fair looking.
His wife staged a Walk-Out on the Too Beautiful Nurse
But I stayed talking with the Lucite tulips.
Their story was so strangely mean-spirited
Maybe it was written by monkeys. Maybe they meant well.
They say a bumble bee won't make it across The Fairway *ever.*
It's too dainty.
It's feminine. He won't take it.
He says a couple of queers over and over and a weirdo.
He calls me The Loner and you New Boy.
I wrote a True Letter. No take-backs.
You better think about a True Letter like that.
People are so disappointed.
Think about something that changed.
Think about something changed
Something at all. Off the bat
The game starts right in the middle.

First surge
Cable

Sounds like a train, a train sounded timeless
coming and going this way

                            children buzz, shedding their skins
               everywhere
                   the TV dove
                   gurgles through walls

someplace it blues the room
it sounds like talking under water
the dove of the cable surge

its divine medicated eye
its full-out melancholy
                   tuned, smoothing
                   the going to sleep dormer
                            hollow-out where the kids are
smoking and sitting their eggs in space

my *Liebestod*

what I heard in the scream blue bag was *heart-flooding*   Horowitz lasting,

watering the keys
I walked in gray worry blankets of politics-the-still

Exquisite   vault   everyone   photographs   proudly

my scream blue bag right there on the deli chair, in the paws of everything closed

Financial
Sunday
I walked in

the morning of the last record, of *Horowitz cry-flooding*

ripping Isolde's *Liebestod* intervals

my blue scream bag cracked open like eggs

Frail of a year

scour-bright singing

despair

after sheens of love's *eye-to-eye kiltering*

misadventure's shock sky

hard-to-bear lyric prancing... *boy, that hurt*

molten

molten, yet in the dry threadbare manner

Midwest

*R*ed nitwit of a building with a façade like classical harmony

> *as I could not now make the love I was*
> *dreams to your*
> bare
> big
> room

with a dull oak floor and windows at the compass
each has
a parchment   blind spreading interior

Bake-off   beet sugars and resentments   the star-studded
> night riding horses

with nothing but steak and tomatoes to prove *what if*

what if this inland
> lake enthusiasm?

soldiering PARTITA

■

why are Gnostic frost, lavender
bedecking the psychic pain

■

I don't know what he's listening to
wired on the cushion, violet head streaming

■

the dream ripped so wrongly
it affronted the query made on the way

■

the answer when I returned was *too much credence soldiering love*
too much fascia off the bone

■

antic
and icon poses

■

a complete train
of chaptered ramshackle,

■

other centuries
crystals benumbing, baffling

■

minute
windows

■

Gnostic frost soldiering too much
love and credence

■

chapter
and train

Little Soulyard, 2

Repute of houses
    liquors and tattoos
        welding
     the saltfix
Tans even
      blue backs
       of the knee
        blue
        elbow
     crooks
The detachment it takes
   a
      frontage
    of cyclone yelling
      grass
     in sheer
Jet Zones
Duchess of piston and rings
      scalloping
     oily
    depressions
Delectations
  of,

Deep Blues
     grass flattens
         the detachment
       it takes
   an ear
     for
Things that fold over
         nature

Sadly, I noticed

there were no strawberries
in the strawberry ice cream
noted for its strawberries

Lost   soft   cloche   with   fake   fur   trim
   Blink faithful   cashmere lost   in the drumming
 in the sandwich board   strike

      2 × dancing: In-the-beginning-joy ------------ then
a spiteful lightfooted
   retaliatory finale   where he takes us all as malice (call
         Kathy and see if
          she's still yearning
      for the strawberry
      Christmas glam
    all the *chinoise*
   fractals

flavorful in their own remembrance
   Pink   the ice cream
    noted
    for its strawberries . . .

Accrual of daft foibles stringing *Logic,* I say   the complete repose of
                                                                nutrition &
                                            antioxidants on the platter
                                                the strawberry heads of pigeons
                                    in   the   air   shaft   relay
                the shock trauma helicopter set down   empty   benign

transit
        possessed   slate   of sky   the final nest   at 80, the two

                                        best things my father said he'd done
in his life: *marrying*

your mother and going to   I say, *I can help you   here let me do tha*t I say,

drier air for the turgid
sinuses are like strawberries

need some help???

I say

but Dad
he takes us all, even the sky *the robin's egg blue equal of angelskin and streaming
marine*

all of us

He takes for malice　　　　I say　　　　*Scottsdale*　　dry air
winking

possessed

slate
of sky
when the locusts start out on the ridges

he says

Ju*st*
Re*doubt*

The Loss　　(*ride with it*)

Andrew, all bespoke

high in the vortex of V or pinnacle, *I continue*
to wreathe
the lie, you remove
the truth

fat grouse of speckles unspelling its design   tray for runneth
and ash
drifting to my pills   *No, Granddaddy, you come with me*

The sill's bowed from fear
the righteous remove from reason

Andrew, whose jabot and puff

the edge of luxury recused from crime
newsy exhales   erotic posting airs on air

up & down
the heart hurt stairs   that Andrew, all bespoke

Eclipse of Effort   That Hurt Form

The Porticos of Toulouse

their crippledom
their bipolar Camels
and sex phone
recall

holstered super tough
throaty crying

chariots of tax flipped on sun
so bored they're begetting
margins
sneakered at the bottom

of turquoise
custodies
archaic rouges
       like *en face* Porticos

       of Toulouse
where the dust motes
and sun
shafts
silhouette
benches
outside

Chambers,

bassoon the reedy camp
to a whole hotel
For Mother
who filigrees their crippledom

polar crying

Porn Guy *Idée Fixe*

[Mother I didn't]   I ran off to practice
frolic of trousers   lime bed survey of the perimeter
dog-eared
viscous   gloss

the door closed the daylights and balcony a kind of geranium
split pendulous
bundled shiny   pawn Crack
bells

pawn crack   [Mother I didn't]
and tempered glass spoils *No wife giveth   Some die foremost*
Bewildered

dominion
of a dear little fetish of First Acts   First Script
unraveling The White Scot
The Fit Bruce

porthole   lookover deigned shoulders   clad-strapped bevy
the porthole
grasps the sea is fat and wicked

blue vein Samothrace wing-blowing
molt verbiage
I read your words,
I'll get back to you,

the LordSmall Years that didn't speak till I was

vanquished   stale blather
gruff   halt
vague *idée*
fixe   [Mother I didn't]

Champagne Blondes / Little Scrap of Irony

Coat like *saran* on the pudding, Blondes

on stems

cool

thin gold marmalade

Blondes

Little Scrap's grass court tortoise

to mascot

the fest

swizzles and buckets

of charm heart

shapes Little Scrap serves

their pendant

sashay

blends

mesh with the wafer cushions

none of the blondes are actually

swimming in

the blue chlorine

secret greenie mold beneath

the lips of the tables

perfect

gist

Ipanema swaddling,

Little Scrap's mugged in the heat and highballs
Blithe *he just stands up to the cedars*
and barbeques gracefully
acres of being and acres
dream
how Little Scrap eludes
the deeper tyrants so successfully
prophylactic
the eunuch of the champagne blondes

The Challenge

They were tragic and flat, they were all attended
Discrete volume, exaggerated leaps
Surpassed by lingering in the apex without descent
No available version but subject/object
Of rings and bracelets shriveled to string, my bag lost
Then no shoes on the platform
They were all tragic and flat, they were but parts
Of the body animate but immobile
Though comforted and fortunately *not shunned*
By manipulations and the sympathies of their masters
Mistresses Pure dependence shriveled in luck they were
Lopped and attended by their loppers also lopped
Or lopping —if I could get out of this back to
The platform even without my shoes, back to the dance
The dancer's complete body, the real streets
Won't sit eggs like revelation's brood
Turned pornography, an exaltation of parts
Head for thought, tooth for chew, grasp of
One ability extended on the universe
One cork haven
Closet haven
Sly tragic collection

59th Street Station

Momentary Aphrodite who takes up the signals and wildness of her own
 race

    to proffer   the ledge
                  rails

                    of the train slithering up   cold good wind
                                        arrived over the fires

Sweet Thing Theology

Mind benumbed or if it's
grace *her entry*
her belfry of décor
thwacks the rushes of
chirping continual ground

here's a cuddle of
sleeping acrobats in
skin tight skin tight

Italian
closest to the musical brain
valence
of buttermouth and dryfall
here, here in the Sun-Katch Raiment

And capes of *THE SHOUTING CUSTOM OF RAIMENT*
wind pines starburst ash
raiment and resins
stuck to
their resting

Benumbed or if it's
grace lashing the rain thwacked
leaves her curlew's
twilight
her phantom enters décor

To the Cinematographer

NOW: *Blue Snows of the Impressionists*

Vegetable domesticity sets small things shining   even the ash-pronged saplings
after the woods are burned, cleared
                                        for livelihood
                                            for research and proving

the clock of bourbon that hands the world its small terror-rose blushing ice
wafers of precinct, an hour (even longer) back to town

                                these fathoms remember . . .
                                    this way blushed . . .

                                    You
                            the man just happened to,

How
you wanted to go someplace and cry things that summed-up,

Here's The Abstract: *Call his sister*

The Pioneer

SEVERE DUST, ALMOST LEADED

rich mustard
fawns on her when the other leaves to talk him out of,

The Text: *bronze, very shiny* range for the part saddled-up, egret pulled sky then a
tense double fuchsia to the bridge   ink whatever you need for it, a stocking for it

     raw
with one floating peach extremely innocent,   puddled, stoved-in

but the Budget Ivory stands where she's eating over the sink the same

ceiling and the ground

the same

High Nouns Shepherd

A Photo is not a True Depiction: the wall back of the stairs
            so close, the foreground
              finial *so* bulbous (verily, the air's
        that much thicker with you
        stored in my
        Red
Sleep)

A Photo obeys notions, not lips of celestial foam . . .
*f*ilm Tar Curls Roiling, still the childproof rubberized
land
escapes

in True Depiction, *real air's thick n' fancy on a plain ride*
like a part of the forest that's shorn
        Thus
            "mudslides of record"
            but not the lambs bleating, snapping like cards
            or you
      hunkered
      in my
      Red
      Sleep
High Nouns Shepherd
the frame twists air

Speak Revenue

THE INSTANT
     I run into you in the makeup brushes sable
lineage of orange Revlon flames
& gold tone Christmas
  the brains of language

"From absolute brutality we will seize men's hats"
the velocities of Czerny, instant
of Desdemona's
LAST
riff
of all holiday lifting the
      "red banners were snapping over
      factories manned by workers"

    & Speak
    Revenue
pressed as Desdemona's pillow before slacking
when she hands the air and palms silverly
Her suzerain to whom fealty's due

mantra

Even the soot-packed walls are planning BIG SWEETS FOR THE
RAGFOOTED
Capriccios . . . .
Delights . . . .
Antics my linden dressed up for   Her role
in the forest
play of brookings and honey drunk
Bees
dirndl Thick

Saga   of
All The Natterings That Wreck Your Grain

Solace Ritual

Before we knew it, eloquence passed.
The days make great pulled efforts   treadless
Unsweet little vials
dry corks crumble and shake a glitter of great crowds
unstartled, unsurprised.
Evening's glue, evening's iconic bonding . . . what about the lanterns noodling time?

How 'bout a strut down the middle of the great glittering crowd?

Sun done yello, then steps back into white
flat and cold there, only a smear of blonde
there in furry trees

the whole of gray arching, creaking, the house is a basket in

Robins prick
sunlight somewhere
trails the yello sing
burn down misting
tuft and clumping

fathers chirping,

daughters,
fair trees. Their soldier martyrs, plus their hills of trip whistling *all out*
yello trills,

Leaves.   Crisping.   The houses behind me stand on
ceremony
horsehair seats
Old running boards of ivory with a drink down the middle, broke and pickets flying
any witch, any moonlight vault

following the voices Spring Bliss Promised

The Dark Dauphine

Four of us marched out singly
to undo a stay of formal delirium, four of us stepped right up to the bar

our charm fell in poems, in the dark like Nita and Zita
we glittered frankly

acorn studded, spidery all-over
       motif's Dauphine
of sunbeam pasties Nita and Zita stitched everywhere

our gullied knees dimpled the bar stools, we snapped our heads and flared
we forgave separately
and shattered one at a time . . . like Nita and Zita did,
                                   artistically

encrusted the dark Dauphine
labeled spigots hot and cold the pair

        Four of us rode a light-made horse and scored a little demented
                 Juliet
               Mandolin
         with heavy-lidded silver

A Letter from Home *To Karen Dalton*

>*She'll die rough*
>>>*and penniless* of raw chance
>>>elide
>>>and forage in the winch

The entire formation of *I fought back*
>>>All over
>>>Viral
>>>Blue
built out the smoke on the mountain

plumbing rents off the wall

her biography's shirt-off-your-back
>>Dowsing

>*I'm sick in the middle*
>>*fold over*
blister and cry

Call Sleeping

We took a bubble bath,
               we licked the Windows
         we'd been talking about Zest Rules
               Take Everything Zest, take
         The Zest For Punishment
               things belong but you have to listen to them Leaving
         Zest We didn't have to listen to
     tragic planes High over the cloud-cover
Zest
     scratch
         we Delighted Completely
               licking
         the windows First
and the things first To Go Well *We Licked!*

The Chiffon Artist

The Gauze Mother

The Solid Object

Lingering in the scrim, The Chiffon Artist
cauls the tray of space

                        and we thirst together, but we moistly
Agree
We've cozied the moment, all tucked in

The cold humming

Beauty

A picture of darling you   barreling emerald eggs *piebald*

Bounded Blue Cushion Grandeur   bounded the medium   punys you resented or

opalized   *When the tide rises all boats float the same*

Unfirm jellies and tactics

Clasp longing right inside its daddy of dragons guarding the door

Hatching skeined drives   nubby sequences

To the dragon edge   the pillow center you had then,

More room than you thought

You had   Less vanity about the brow

Mandarin Character,
YELLO CROWN

I wold tak her w/ me She's the one

reads spirits quietly   talks to them,

                  so I'd tak her for safety and for love

flutters   their time of fringe-wisp depths   tak her

TO Find TO Read   the Mandarin Character from the top down   drawn subtly

                      alive whitely

        as owls bloodstreaking dinner on high

When shadows walked darkness forward I'd xplain

                  a tortoise is breaking up in flames   in sections

                        split so . . .

I'd tak her the buttercup   tak her the yello crown spying pollens of simulacra

                teary tail-biting Circles   Logic

the ground comes right out from under   if the soul hasn't got any gender

              then   what was he fighting FOR

                     BEFORE

          disappeared?   completely ?

I wold tak her the buttercup and crown
to circle the   immune
        Grandiflora
     Lush
to arrive at a word

Water Quip

to Lois Hirshkowitz

Piqué and restive
to the water   lowboxed mourning to the kitchen level striation she's walking to the little
Pantheon of the sea,

Water Quip

Luscious morphing under arm lift 'twixt getting up, getting around

Her
and the all of pandering
creaming world crush,
sibilant
mirror   life,
gilled other
breathing
Forward
swarming

close guardian to the water poise and   bug-eyed languish
anti-headstone   anti-monument

flux she digged down,
discarding backward at the flange of dress-arms,

deviled in canopy
&
billow
to the water

piqué right up
to
pour her profile hair
her lash-whipped   buckets to the gossiping, bickering fountain

Poem on Velvet & Fire's Extra Fun

Everybody's swooning and the fat free dancers (so beautiful in sorrow) believe a perfect
circle

Everybody believes the tendentious rouster rattling down the back stairs

will make his candidate
Rebar, everything in train

Set out pronged obelisks

glow and burnish

.

This house is its own Mesopotamia, shaping flacons, teasing the juices out of the eye

the high-handed concierge
is a swell of bony finish skimming

grids of capture,

■

But who wants near the baseboard orange -------- fire black runnels? You can't play in fire
or goad its demons, no matter what
                             Fire rents the dust wallet for fire's extra fun
                             and Glory

takes off screaming I don't want to feel or see by
fire
burning all the talent papers
                             fire won't hear

djinns in orbit

I was seeing the dragonfly score the temple following silence
inside
djinns in orbit clustered light
the temple-bidden highstep goosestep
crunching silence
inside
somebody's recessed slippers the outside women cocooning
jewelling milk squealing babies
outside the temple's flame-swung triparte
sacred geometry built on the inside
rose of the unseen
paycock writ daily
in and out stacked grains and kernels lay down in the numerous
absorbing pitch
infinity stretch
the temple the dragonfly's crossing buzzes
rupestral whites

14 lines

facts stumble narrow stairs
periscope to cloud superior
above the swimming dark unnamable figures waltz

volume   metric   this much remains
mere invalid
crabbing living

wandering the car garage the warehouse silvers
wandering the predicate
of a stalwart order

metrics bully
the invalid remains

her cloud of light through the gray sky
script of her
cursive remains

2 hands writing

Cursive as Cadillac
    Lanes the hand beautifully, dutifully
as *Islam sans effigy.* A wind-up case
        of fast tendrils hard to read till one's *absorbed*
disciplined to this style of the sleek
        yodeling pages. Forthwith diesel
rocket fuel, mud and water.
        Grit polished out
for a few translucent pieces

Old World Lyric
        of the cup in the clouds roiling
capitals and fishing under the water line
        Symphonic quill . . . ink on the lips
honing banners of "r"
        "T" that's the instinct for following instinct
navigating, stamping, misting "O"
        all around
its yeasty *legerdemain* and wick

Blue Hour

of mi*nute*
gliding

hour nostalgic, not for time
but time's
clemency circles
the belly
the fiery abdomen

hurt for seeds

Blue Hour's haste
drives ahead
candles
the path on the way
that makes doves blind

& curves like margrave
views, like The Doge
marrying sea froth
paddocks
& funnels of Findhorn

Vikings scathed

order
blue
at the last hour of purchase
fragment
wage

Great Expectations

If you was 50 Pips enriching me had perished

Bread and butter was gone

Great black pall, trenchant for the fugitive shuddering nettles in both arms

Meat bone for the misty

Rimy morning *You have got the ague,* said I

If some goblin as iron riveted to listen

Pudding was on the boil at the first punishing amen at this dismal time

What light we had

What way we could

Struck out, slipped off Gravesend . . . rowed, rowed and rowed

"Do you, dear boy?" a sort of Sunday tune

I was a'growing rich

For any mastering idea meant to lie all night by

Skiffs and wherries briskly constant for any mastering idea

The road that ran crisp for Hamburg

For Rotterdam "Is he there?" said

Herbert, summer in the light,

Winter in shade as iron was riveted, he was already mincemeat down

The sign of the house caged and threatened

My benefactor driving down irresistibly

A meat bone for the mighty marshes

My place while he lived

Great North
Primitive Story

I wish I were there. With you.
in my therefore bed
thin-walls tottering, I could be The Narrows

Channel
to the other side

Scot Stands the World Eye
white slaps storming,   votive, demure   tartan
as crossed woods in fire,
eyes troubled empty
braying, rocking clipping the log light,
the great quiet
Great North

Breath huffing
basalt
cupping mollusks, skirling trees   but Gliding *I was there with you*
to race
the border,
and sea spray youth,

Over and Over I begged all the chores and the efficiencies

I'm feeling

the shoulders

of

your hair streaming now, dying down   now
Great North with her Cold

Primitive

feeling the shoulders of

Bread Alone

Haystacks gloaming in the sunset most high
                                       astride all glowing spirituals

The knapsack and it load-doubled wanderer
                           at the edge of hunger called passion

Groaning piers in such yello green water
                           are the loading docks of old form

And the turbulent top where waves trade collapse
                         have borrowed a bottomed custody

Crackling headrests of tombs underfoot
                         beetles scrabble and crunch

Small green fires trouble the hands
                         vein riven barter and warmth

Walk About emptying this much is the dare
                         spiraling off the glass highway

Corrugated ruins of snarling doors
                         are sliver jars of infinity

And haystacks gloaming in the sunset most high
                         and stutters that surf against breaking

Poem on Velvet, Carnegie Hall

The double bass Chair is nodding the cornice and flags the riser

these boxes have red lips and The Weaver's gold warps

woof woof Duke's nude piano black glass

both drums tilted

search for women   they Sinatra each other *if he still matters*

Rachmaninoff Goodman

Garland heartskipping Vladimir's fish and the wine-tabbed chairs

flip ditties: Baker, Josephine

welling

Photographing us with cell phones the viola is, and the clarinet is the orchestra is

pouring kettles and squirrelly guts of horned

Callas bouffant, Flatt & Scruggs Rubenstein

The Cleveland

The Beatles

peradventure Ella's highwire

peradventure Holiday's flume

Van Cliburn alighting and the whole world is tune

Floating Island

the glider thrusts to Zinnia's Mexico
bright squeaking

meandering springs
piquant fix

atop the mechanism
on the smooth tiles

uneasy keeps
day on the glider goes

deeper
sashays

and climbs
slung in its own felt reach

Red Sleep

It has happened
the bricks fell off their protection, hitting me
red baked in rooms
cold for a machine diagnostic
it happened through suave clowns, field notes dangling
marginalia
victims
posh as banks once were ripping sudden death
shutdown all for itself *Shutdown*
any crying for its own
gnawed fathom
Red Sleep
strips
those titans   now they get fingered at the first arched brow of power
in red
tender rest

WIDOW   on a train

          Could   I   be   fantastical, *sheer*

          Knobbed   with a may be side ways face

     festive with   gourds   skirted with iguanas like fringe

     A   Solid   Curtain

of my separate

Vertical Fears

          I could enchant a Beautiful Day in The Republic

                              Quietest   Car

                              of Finest   Nouns

          & generate   *Reserve*   Measure & Lure

                    Fellowship   like   lilacs   in   their   sandy

     but   could I just be holding

     my handout

like   a claw to South Philly

rooftop caves breaking their sides in beige solution,

                but could   I   be   Some Cerulean Fantasy   Orb

green

    lips

                massaged   on   a   train

Outside's

tender

none of the pranks of void   a furred sizzling
                a murmured

& *outside is also*   *a creature hunching his comma*

his fervid glyph bells the roof
              leaf in the crowned body of the martyred lack

       tenderly in the dark
         pitch

             Here's my birdcage thin brass *cantoring*
gibberish cracks the backs of

        His comma
His fervid glyph   & spine

of the riser's barnacle iron

          outside's

    tawny
   softly in itself

over the sharp dandelion shovel leaves

       outside's cottony   puffed over the tracks

Baby Krishna crawls to bliss

The Lounges are grape leaf thick, their waxy hands long loving
Incarnations
Sag in rattan

The first mantra of the day is: *GANESH WITH HIS MOUSE FOOTMEN*

Then, *BABY KRISHNA CRAWLS TO BLISS*
                            the Lionhearted
                                wisdom loving wisdom's
                    Granite Spar

                                    even in the crosshairs

Baby Krishna crawls to bliss

The Banjo Clock

HOUR ON THE HOUR *the cream must have some yello in it to strum*
in the arms of the Magus in Titian teal
a great moon front of sky

this street won't happen again   this term, this avenue gestures
lindens and Spring   the moon with its small-engine-dark-blue-falling back in its
hum right here's the lumber   the gang box   the eggs for coddling superstition

       without naming the fractures or cleaves of repetition
                            descry the buttonhole stars'
gassy wisps

galactic hours little green minutes ding and tick   the countryside, Zola said,
looks cut up   looks like beetles grind its leaves
pinch and masticate all soft skin

the moon shouts mad despair
keep walking
used to the sound

of moist emotion   the smoother attributes   saint blarney and futile crime
the melancholy sadists of the Rhineland talk
the aftertaste

       afternoon wheel scrapes toss boxes of squeal
the headlights cold halogen streams a watery exchange,

diffuse as the banjo moon *has a little yello in it*
in the arms of the Magus in his Titian teal
nevertheless capacity,

strums the whole ground of light and hollow
true chiaroscuro
like Rembrandt stepped right out of the psalms

Acknowledgments

with gratitude to the editors of publications in which the following poems appeared:

Aufgabe 9: "Beauty," "Gorge," "Water Quip"

Barrow Street (winter 2009): "The Banjo Clock"

Cannibal, no. 2: "Island of the Judge who kept us"

Caliban online, no. 5: "my *Liebestod*"

Denver Quarterly 41, no. 2: "Bear"

Fence 11, no. 1 (spring/summer 2008): "Ikebana" (from "LORD BALTIMORE *the Musical*")

Lana Turner 1: "*Fanta grape,*" "*Eternal Youth,*" "Mandarin Character, YELLO CROWN," "Great Expectations"

Lana Turner 2: "*Call Sleeping,*" "The Dark Dauphine," "High Nouns Shepherd," "*Speak Revenue*"

New American Writing 24: "The Chiffon Artist," "The Porticos of Toulouse"

New American Writing 27: "Sweet Thing Theology"

POOL 6: "Buckle up, Sweetie"

VOLT: The War Issue, War Number: "National sky"

Zoland Poetry 5: "First surge Cable," "59th Street Station"

With love to New York City, still everyplace at once. To the Northeast Corridor on trains, the man with the harem, and all these people I get to see. I kiss Minch. Love to all the sustaining texts with their body and heft.

Notes

Epigraph: from "What is it o'clock? Or the door (we never enter)," translated from the French by Catherine A. F. MacGillivray in Hélène Cixous's *Stigmata: Escaping Texts*.

"Bear": the final rhyming stanza is from Abraham Lincoln's poem "The Bear Hunt."

"Speak Revenue": italicized lines by F. T. Marianetti, Italian Futurist, is from *Manifesto, A Century of Isms,* edited by Mary Ann Caws.

"The Dark Dauphine": Nita and Zita were sisters who came to America from Eastern Europe in the 1920s. Exotic dancers in Theda Bara mode, they toured extensively before settling in New Orleans. Nita and Zita sewed and embroidered their own clothing and costumes. In a distinctively dense Turkish manner, they decorated everything, including the walls and fixtures of their home on Dauphine St.

"A Letter from Home *To Karen Dalton*": Karen Dalton (1937–1993) was a singer who played a long neck banjo.

"Great Expectations": is composed from lines from *Great Expectations* by Charles Dickens.

"The Banjo Clock": final line adapted from Malraux on Rembrandt in *The Voices of Silence,* translated by Stuart Gilbert.

NEW CALIFORNIA POETRY

edited by	Robert Hass
	Calvin Bedient
	Brenda Hillman
	Forrest Gander

For, by Carol Snow

Enola Gay, by Mark Levine

Selected Poems, by Fanny Howe

Sleeping with the Dictionary, by Harryette Mullen

Commons, by Myung Mi Kim

The Guns and Flags Project, by Geoffrey G. O'Brien

Gone, by Fanny Howe

Why/Why Not, by Martha Ronk

A Carnage in the Lovetrees, by Richard Greenfield

The Seventy Prepositions, by Carol Snow

Not Even Then, by Brian Blanchfield

Facts for Visitors, by Srikanth Reddy

Weather Eye Open, by Sarah Gridley

Subject, by Laura Mullen

This Connection of Everyone with Lungs, by Juliana Spahr

The Totality for Kids, by Joshua Clover

The Wilds, by Mark Levine

I Love Artists, by Mei-mei Berssenbrugge

Harm., by Steve Willard

Green and Gray, by Geoffrey G. O'Brien

The Age of Huts (compleat), by Ron Silliman

Selected Poems, 1974–2006: it's go in horizontal, by Leslie Scalapino

rimertown/an atlas, by Laura Walker

Ours, by Cole Swensen

Virgil and the Mountain Cat: Poems, by David Lau

Sight Map: Poems, by Brian Teare
Transcendental Studies: A Trilogy, by Keith Waldrop
R's Boat, by Lisa Robertson
Green is the Orator, by Sarah Gridley
Writing the Silences, by Richard O. Moore
Voyager, by Srikanth Reddy
Dark Archive, by Laura Mullen
Metropole, by Geoffrey O'Brien
The Banjo Clock, by Karen Garthe
In the Bee Latitudes, by 'Annah Sobelman
Gravesend, by Cole Swensen

Text and display Garamond Premier Pro   *Compositor* BookMatters, Berkeley
Printer and binder Maple-Vail Book Manufacturing Group

■